# The Just Price Of Flowers

**a play by James Yarker
with lyrics by Craig Stephens
after Bertolt Brecht**

ISBN 978-1-913185-06-0

Published by Stan's Cafe
Birmingham, UK
2020

www.stanscafe.co.uk

The Just Price Of Flowers © James Yarker 2009
Song Lyrics © Craig Stephens 2009
Photos © Graeme Braidwood 2012
Publication © Stan's Cafe 2020

www.ingramcontent.com/pod-product-compliance
Lightning Source LLC
Chambersburg PA
CBHW071756080526
44588CB00013B/2256

**About the illustration and design**

The illustrations for the covers of these books were undertaken by students at Birmingham City University as the final module of their first-year illustration course during the Spring/Summer of 2018. The images were developed through workshops using variations of the theatre-devising methods employed by Stan's Cafe but adapted and applied to the making of visual work. The resulting work was shown in the pop-up exhibition *The Something Of Somebody Something* at Stan's Cafe's venue @AE Harris in May 2018.

The design concept of the books was produced by final year Graphic Design student Aimee Chapman. These were then further developed for print in a collaborative process between Stan's Cafe and the University's Innovation Product Support Service (IPSS) which involved helping the company to select appropriate DTP software, undertaking training and selecting a suitable print on demand service.

Gareth Courage
Lecturer in Illustration
Birmingham City University

| | |
|---|---|
| Script: | James Yarker |
| Lyrics: | Craig Stephens |
| Music: | Brian Duffy |
| Accordion Transposition: | Jill Dowse |
| Origami 2009 & 2011: | Brian Duffy |
| Origami 2012: | Harry Trow |
| Stage Management 2012: | Harry Trow |
| Lighting Design 2009 & 2011: | Stan's Cafe |
| Lighting Design 2012: | Simon Bond |
| Set: | Stan's Cafe |
| Costumes: | Stan's Cafe with Kay Wilton |
| Direction: | James Yarker Craig Stephens & Amanda Hadingue |
| Producer: | Charlotte Martin |

The Just Price Of Flowers was written after reading
House Of Cards by William D Cohan
and
Tulipmania by Anne Goldgar

**Credits**

3 - 5 December 2009
@ A.E.Harris

| | |
|---|---|
| Florist: | Christine Dugrenier |
| Husband: | Kerrie Reading |
| Wife: | Charlotte Gregory |
| Banker: | Bharti Patel |
| Worker: | Lucy Nicholls |
| Financier: | Craig Stephens |
| Narrator: | Amanda Hadingue |

6 March 2011
Warwick Arts Centre

| | |
|---|---|
| Florist: | Amanda Hadingue |
| Husband: | Jack Trow |
| Wife: | Charlotte Gregory |
| Banker: | Bernadette Russell |
| Worker: | Gerard Bell |
| Financier: | Craig Stephens |

15 - 30 June 2012
@ A.E.Harris
12 July 2012
Latitude Festival, Southwold
-Co-produced by Birmingham Repertory Theatre

| | |
|---|---|
| Florist: | Valerie Cutko |
| Husband: | Jack Trow |
| Wife: | Charlotte Gregory |
| Banker: | Bernadette Russell |
| Worker: | Gerard Bell |
| Financier: | Craig Stephens |
| Narrator: | Jill Dowes |

Financier: I've done my best in difficult circumstances. You can't buck the market. To a certain extent it comes down to luck and we have been unlucky with the timing.

Worker: *We've* been unlucky? it's my pension we're talking about!

Financier: I have a considerable investment in the same fund.

Worker: And what are you doing about that?

Financier: I'm just hanging on in there. It will all come good in time, it's a cycle, I plan to ride out this down turn and I suggest you do the same.

Worker: What?

Financier: In two or three years I expect the value of your pension to be back where we had hoped it would be.

Worker: You want me to continue working for another two or three years?

Financier: The choice is yours.

Worker: It doesn't seem like I have a choice... that I ever had any choice at all.

[Song Reprise]

Narrator: The tulip in its healthy state takes on a form that pleases
Yet how much more exotic when mutated by diseases
Riddled with contagion it 'breaks' with flames divine
Prized beyond all reason I wish that it was mine

All: Yes you see we all have human needs
Some are basic and some bring you to your knees.

Worker: What?

Financier: That this final payment sum is not guaranteed, it relies on the market, it pays what the market rate is at the time of maturity, unless you choose to extend that point.

Worker: And the time of maturity is next month.

Financier: Yes and at this time the market is particularly weak, the weakest I can recall. If you cash in next month I fear you will get very poor returns.

Worker: But, I don't understand. I've been buying a pension not investing in the tulip madness.

Financier: What do you think I've been doing with your money to try and get the growth you need?

Worker: Gambling it!

Financier: No! If I had just lent it out and waited for it to collect interest, with other prices always rising? Your savings would be worth next to nothing by now if I had done that.

Worker: And now you're telling me my pension is worth next to nothing it sounds like I'm in that position anyway.

Financier: It's just bad luck.

Worker: Not for you! You take your cut no matter what happens to my money.

Financier: You expect to be paid for the work you do, why shouldn't I?

Worker: I don't expect to be paid if I totally fail to do what I say I will do.

Wife: It looks like he won from any angle we look at it from.

Florist: Yes, he played a bad hand very well.

Wife: He took a big cut of our money because he said he was taking great risks.

Husband: But it was our money he was risking.

Wife: He took big cuts because he was making so much money for us.

Husband: But where is that money, where has it gone?

### Scene 21: The Pension (pt 2)
Financier and Worker [Financier's Office]

*In which Worker finds he can't retire after all.*

Narrator: Scene 21: In which the FTSE 100 index continues to fall.

Worker: There you are Mr. Van Tage, the very final payment into that pension of mine. One hundred percent, right to the end, as I'd always promised. I wasn't going to let trouble with the Van Leasings spoil that record was I. I will see you next month for the payout then. It will have been a pleasure and that is the last you will see of me.

Financier: Mr. Van Driver wait. Please come back. There is some news that I think you may find unpleasant. Won't you please sit down. May I have someone get you something, a drink perhaps, hot, cold, stiff?

Worker: No thank you. Please say what it is you have to say?

Financier: Your pension. You do understand how it works don't you? It was all explained to you by my father when your first began was it not?

| | |
|---|---|
| | the market I expect. We put more love into them than people are prepared to pay for. |
| Wife: | You do still love them though don't you? Even though they've lost you a fortune. |
| Florist: | Of course I do, they are still the same flower. They have the same beauty. They haven't lost me anything. What about you, do you still love them? |
| Wife: | I'm not sure I ever did. |
| Husband: | I did, but I can hardly bear to look at them now. Why didn't we sell at the height? |
| Florist: | The failed investor's eternal question. |
| Wife: | It turns out you don't know the height until you are looking back up at it from below. |
| Husband: | How low. |
| Florist: | If everyone won then there would be no winners. It is the losers who create the winners. |
| Wife: | Did you win Mr. Van Eeek? |
| Husband: | Of course he did. |
| Van Eeek: | I suppose I did, in a small way. I spent as much time getting out of the trade as I did getting in. You see I am a Florist not a Financier. For me the profit is subsidiary to the bloom, I sold more than I bought. I grew more than I spent. |
| Wife: | Van Hire, he won, but I don't know how. |
| Florist: | He didn't lose, which for him, in the circumstances, must be considered a victory. |

**Scene 20: Old Money**
Wife, Husband, Florist [Florist's Garden]

In which, destitute, Husband and Wife work for Florist
and admire his tulips.

Narrator: Scene 20: In which Ted Bateman takes part time work with his wife stacking shelves in Morrisons.

[Wife and Husband scrub the floor whilst Florist admires a tulip]

Husband: Mr. Van Eeek. How much was this garden worth when everything was at its height?

Florist: I never really calculated it, but, I don't know, one, two hundred thousand guilders.

Wife: And now?

Florist: I really don't know. How much are the plants in anyone's garden worth?

More here than they would be if we took them down to

for you. To keep you honest. There has to be a down side as well as an up side. And if we were to save him who would pay us, where would all the money come from for that? He would need to straighten out his asset book and who would pay that money? It would need, potentially, everyone in the land to give him a thousand guilders. I cannot see how this possible. [Both look out to the audience]

### Scene 19; The Rescue Package
Banker [At Home]

In which Banker is bailed out by governments.

Narrator: Scene 19: in which Sir Fred Goodwin retires on his pension.

Banker : [Sits alone on stage eating a large cream cake]

Financier: But there was leverage at each stage. What were you on 5, 7, 10 guilder's loaned for each guilder of security and that squared, 25, 49, 100 guilders to one!

Banker: And you haven't done the same?

Financier That hurts Van hire.

Florist: Now the contagion has spread, less than prime has become poisonous and AAA is now single B at best.

Financier: You had hedges?

Banker: Not enough for this. Do you? Do you? Listen, this isn't my problem; it's your problem. I've been trying to sell these [I.O.U. bundles] discreetly for days. I've finally found someone who will have some of them, but at prices too low to contemplate. I sell at those prices and all your equivalent holdings are marked down. Your assets values are slashed. You look terrible on paper and in the flesh. Do you want me to do that? People see me fall and they lose confidence in you. They lose confidence in you and they ask you to repay what you owe, in a hurry, can you cope with that? Can you? Today I fall tomorrow you fall. And after you then you, then another, one by one or in clusters and who knows where it will end? I do; The Dark Ages.

Florist: Blackmail!

Banker: Economics.

Financier: If you will excuse us. [Financier and Florist huddle downstage]

Florist: He must be allowed to fail. If he doesn't fail then what will stop him or anyone else from building up all those crazy loans again? It will cost me, heaven knows I will take a beating, but we need there to be a downside for him and

Financier: We don't care about other people or how it is done, we need our money.

Banker: Well...

Florist: We are influential people.

Financier: Bad men to make angry.

Florist: Fail to pay us then you are toast, semolina, fried, totally screwed.

Financier: Totally screwed fried semolina on toast.

Banker: Listen. You know I am a man of good faith.

Financier: And bad debt. You should have been more thrifty Van Hire.

Banker: I just need more time. I have the assets but converting them into cash is difficult. People have been defaulting on these. [Shakes a bundle of I.O.U.s]

Financier: I don't think you do have the assets, not any more.

Florist: What security did you have behind those?

Banker: These. [Shakes a different bundle of I.O.U.s]

Florist: The same things?

Banker: No!

Financier: I.O.U. bundles squared!

Banker: No, no, no. Those were less than prime quality loans I admit, but the securities were rated AAA, they were qualitatively different.

Worker: Where is the justice in this? The world's not right. [exits]

Banker: He's not happy but a contract is a contract.

Financier: And he has no idea how much worse it's going to get.

### Scene 18: Moral Hazard
Banker, Financier and Florist [Banker's Office]

In which Banker claims he is too big to fail.

Narrator: Scene 18: in which Jean's business, with four employees, fails as he can find no bank willing to help him resolve cash flow problems.

Florist: Do you have my money Van Hire?

Financier: I have redemptions due too that I wish to reclaim, do you have those?

Banker: I'm afraid we have a problem. To be candid, too many of my investors are claiming their money at once and I can't raise enough guilders fast enough to satisfy them all. Liquidating fast without it looking like a fire-sale is difficult.

Worker: Yes it was.

Banker: You took it from their house!

Worker: They owed me two months wages and said they weren't be able to pay, so this seemed like fair exchange.

Banker: The Van Leasings owe me money too and I have a binding legal agreement that says in the event of their defaulting on my loan that peacock belongs to me. So hand it over.

Worker: No way! What did you do to earn this?

Banker: I've told you. I leant them money. We had an agreement. That's mine.

Worker: And what did I do? I made them breakfast and dinner, scrubbed their house, their dishes, their clothes. I cleared grates and laid fires. I tended their garden. I danced attendance on their dogs and bless'd bulbs. It was my only job, my only source of income and for two months I haven't been paid.

You lend them some money and sit on your arse and you think that your claim to this peacock is greater than mine? I do not share your map of the world Mr Van Hire, not at all!

Financier: Van Driver, Mr Van Hire is right. Your claim on the peacock is subservient to his. He has the paperwork on his side, you have nothing but a grievance on yours. I would advise you to hand over the peacock, unless you feel it worth going to gaol for.

Worker: This is not right, not right at all. It can't be!

Banker: Hand it over, unless you wish to meet with my lawyers.

Banker: And yet it makes sense Van Tage. Combined we would be so much more than the sum of our strengths. My savings and loan experience; your eye for an investment and opportunity; my clients; your contacts: it's attractive is it not? Van Hire and Van Tage, Hire and Tage. We can work the details out later.

Financier: It won't happen Joost, no matter what you say. I don't want your loan book or creditors.

Banker: Maybe you're right, maybe fifty fifty doesn't reflect the relative size of our operations. Maybe it's sixty forty in your favour.

Financier: You flatter yourself I feel.

Banker: If you want to play hardball I'll buy you out! I'll buy your business. I'll raise a loan. I'll use the business itself as security. You won't be able to do anything about it. I'll be happy to employ you as an advisor of course, you could use your own office of course and keep the perks,

Financier: You are a fantasist Van Hire.

Banker: OK, you win seventy to thirty in your favour but I keep my house and preside as non-Executive Chairman. Please Adrian, please I'm not begging you but please!

[Worker crosses upstage holding the peacock]

Banker: Oi! Stop. What's your name, Van Driver. Come back!

Worker: Sir?

Banker: That peacock?

Worker: Yes.

Banker: It's from the Van Leasings is it not?

|         | Eeek. I owe you nothing until then. So kindly leave. |
|---------|---|
| Florist: | Very well, but I will back tomorrow for that money and every redemption day thereafter for the rest.    [Exits] |
| Banker: | Van Eeek you can't pull it all! |
| Worker: | You know, they maybe both priceless and worthless but they are not useless. They're ready cut to size for wiping shit from one's arse. |

### Scene 17: Leveraged Buyout (failed)
Banker, Financier and Worker [A Cafe]

In which Banker tries to cash in his insurance.

| Narrator: | Scene 17: In which Halifax and Bank of Scotland merge and Mrs O'Reagan is none the wiser. |
|---|---|
| Financier: | Ha ha, very good Van Hire! No one could critique your sense of optimism or the absurd. |

Florist: I can't find Van Ish anywhere, he seems to have disappeared. No one else will touch them with a dyke jumping pole. I'm afraid, to use a quaint English phrase, "you are lumbered with them, mate".

Banker: Maybe I should be buying up other people's at rock-bottom prices. Now is the time to be aggressive, to seize the opportunity!

Florist: Do you have any money?

Banker: Liquidity is at a premium.

Florist: Do you have any money?

Banker: As I say, currently, due to market conditions…

Florist: Do you have my money? I want back the money you owe me.

Banker: Come now Van Eeek there's no need for that.

Florist: It is my money, I want it back.

Banker: I was hoping that we could extend our current arrangement on similar terms.

Florist: This morning I may have considered an extension at a higher rate, but now, after my tour with those things, my rating of you has declined. B at best.

Worker: Who'd credit it? No one, it would seem.

Banker: Single B. Van Eeek you will kill me.

Florist: That is not my concern. I want my money back. If I do not get it you will look back on Single B with fondness.

Banker: Your first redemption date is not until tomorrow Van

### Scene 16: Toxic Assets
Banker, Florist and Worker [Banker's Office]

In which Banker is told his I.O.U.s have no value.

Narrator: Scene 16: in which Alistair Darling is accused of talking the market down.

Worker: Everything alright sir?

Banker: [vacantly] Yes fine. Market conditions are challenging, with second quarter profits expected to be sharply down on last year's record highs, but looking ahead we are expecting consolidation in the third quarter with a strengthening position coming into year-end.

Worker: Which means you're doomed?

Banker: No, not at all! I refute that accusation entirely. It's that kind of scaremongering, talking down the market, that is ill-informed, unhelpful, and ultimately unpatriotic!

Florist: [arrives and tosses a bundle of I.O.U.s to Banker] They're priceless.

Banker: [to Worker] See! [to Florist] Really?

Florist: Yes, absolutely priceless. I cannot get anyone to give me a price on them. They are worthless.

Worker: Both priceless and worthless!

Florist: You can only get a price if someone is willing to buy and if no one is willing to buy then it is without price and therefore worthless.

Banker: Surely someone has some interest in buying them. What about Van Ish?

Wife: The rest is gone.

Banker: Where?

Husband: Nowhere, it's just vanished.

Banker: But that was thousands and thousands of guilders.

Husband: We didn't mean to.

Banker: I can't believe… hold on, where's the peacock?
Give me the peacock.

Wife: We can't.

Banker: Give me my peacock.

Husband: One of the other creditors took it...

Banker: Give me my peacock.

Husband: ...when the house was repossessed.

Wife: We don't have it. We don't have anything.

Banker: GIVE ME MY PEACOCK!
GIVE ME MY PEACOCK!
GIVE ME MY PEACOCK!

[Husband and Wife exit]

I WILL DESTROY YOU.
YOU WILL NEVER BE WORTH ANYTHING IN THIS TOWN AGAIN.
YOU WILL BE MY SLAVES FOR LIFE!

**Scene 15: Bankruptcy**
Banker, Wife and Husband [Bankers Office]

In which Wife and Husband tell Banker they are Bankrupt
and the Banker goes nuts.

Narrator: Scene 15: In which Sean, gets his car repossessed and can no longer get to work.

[Husband and Wife stand side by side. Banker's jaw is slack open]

Husband: We're sorry Mr. Van Hire, it all… went wrong.

Wife: This is yours [she hands over a flower]. There are hundreds of bulbs in the ground. We've sold many but the rest are yours. Here's the list, what the bulb is, how much it weighed, whose garden it is in and where in that garden it is planted.

Husband: Now this belongs to you [hands over the ring].
and these [they take off and hand over their ruffs].
But that's all we have.

| | |
|---|---|
| All: | Yes you see we all have human needs |
| | Some are basic and some bring you to your knees. |
| | |
| Wife: | We all need help from time to time if things aren't going well |
| | We all need someone to care for us when we are feeling ill |
| Banker: | We all need time to relax a little, kick back and have some fun |
| | And we all need space to sit and think of what one day we could become. |
| | |
| Husband: | We all need a special place to go, somewhere where we belong |
| | We all need a chance to take a chance and sometimes get it wrong |
| Florist: | We all need to win a prize just once, to be told that we're number one. |
| | And we all need someone to hold our hand and remember us when we're gone. |
| | |
| Worker: | But some need more than these few things they are never satisfied |
| | They long to have just one more thing or something that is better |
| Various: | Caviar, and pate foie gras and a cellar of fine French wine |
| | They need a large detached with separate garage and several bathrooms |
| All: | They need to have the whitest teeth, the latest suit and hat |
| | They need to have the fastest car, the biggest this and that |
| | Their picture in every magazine for everyone to see |
| | They need to be at the top of the tree looking down on you and me. |
| | |
| | Yes you see, we all have human needs |
| | Some are basic and some bring you to your knees. |

[Song]

| | |
|---|---|
| Narrator: | A human being has many needs |
| | Yes we are needy beings |
| | And before you say not me, not I |
| | Before you all deny it |
| + Wife: | Please listen to what we have to say |
| | And then make up your mind |
| | And then make up your own mind |

+ Fin: We all need water to quench our thirst and food to fill our guts
We all need a home to rest our bones and clothes to keep us warm
We all need work to earn some cash and make us feel worthwhile
We all need a friend to lend an ear and share our hopes and dreams.

Wife: Eight hundred.

Financier: [mock aghast, laughing, turns to go]

Wife: Seven fifty.

Financier: Have you been watching the market?

Wife: Yes and eight hundred is a just price.

Financier: It may have been when you checked last night, but that's not so this morning. This morning six hundred would be generous.

Wife: I can't sell for that. We paid much more than that for it just yesterday morning.

Financier: [shrugs]

Wife: Seven hundred.

Financier: I don't really need it until late tomorrow. I will come back and buy it then, when the price has halved.

Wife: You won't, you won't! I'll sell it to someone else.

Financier: [looks around] You can try. [moves to leave]

Wife: Do you want to buy any of our other flowers?

Financier: No, that is the only one that interests me. I will come back tomorrow and buy it for three.

## Scene 14: Short Selling (pt 3)
Financier & Wife [The Flower Market]

In which Wife nearly sells a cheap flower to Financier.

Narrator: Scene 14: In which, losing at Monopoly, Edward (aged 10) throws the board in the air, storms off to his room and misses out on supper.

[Financier and Wife are discussing a tulip, which she is holding]

Financier: A Emperor Julius III, unless I am mistaken.

Wife: It is.

Financier: And a very fine specimen.

Wife: It is.

Financier: Is it for sale?

Wife: Yes, if the price is right.

Financier: What are you asking?

miss the top end of profit but too late and your capital is down the canal.

Financier: How much do you think this is worth?

Husband: The Emperor Julius III? Now, with the rain we've had, ten minutes left on the day's trading, with the national psyche as it is? I'd give you a thousand guilders for it.

Financier: Only a thousand! But I paid one thousand two hundred guilders for it just two days ago!

Husband: Well there you are you see, that's what I was saying. If you excuse me, you were done.

Financier: Done?

Husband: They saw you coming. Yes the price has eased off in the last few days but it was never worth twelve hundred. I'm sorry.

Financier: But you would give me a thousand?

Husband: It's the best I can do. That's the rate. I have my costs, the people that lend me money.

Financier: Fine. I am clearly not cut out for this flower trade. As you say I had better get out early and minimise my losses.

Husband: Very wise.

Husband: Yes, really know what's what.

Financier: I suppose so.

Husband: Oh yes, you need to be really close to the action or you're lost.

Financier: Are you?

Husband: Oh yes, if you're not in the know you're nowhere. Show any sign of weakness and they'll eat you alive.

Financier: Who?

Husband: The Bulls (or is it the Bears?) Whoever it is they're utterly ruthless.

Financier: Really?

Husband: Oh yes, you mustn't blink or they'll turn on you, you'll be done for.

Financier: You sound knowledgeable.

Husband: Oh yes, yes. I'm a tulip merchant myself.

Financier: Really!

Husband: Yes, yes, just in a small way you understand. I used to be an undertaker so it knew about flowers. It was a seamless transition.

Financier: I see.

Husband: The key thing is not to be stuck with stock you can't sell.

Financier: [aside] Or bodies you can't bury.

Husband: Better to sell too soon than too late. Too early and you

**Scene 13**
Financier & Husband [The Flower Market]

In which Husband buys what he thinks is a cheap flower from Financier.

Narrator: Scene 13: In which Ralf Cioffi and Matthew Tannin are put on trial for insider trading and later acquitted.

Husband: An Emperor Julius III, unless I am mistaken.

Financier: Is it?

Husband: Yes, and a very fine specimen.

Financier: I don't really know anything about flowers, in fact I don't quite know why I bought it. People said it was a good investment, but I don't think I'm really cut out for this trade.

Husband: You have to know what you're doing.

Financier: I suppose you do.

|  |  |
|---|---|
|  | prices of tulips slip back a little. |
| Financier: | But Van Hire still merits double A? |
| Florist: | He knows what he is doing. |
| Financier: | You think prices will fall but you are not considering selling your stock of tulips? |
| Florist: | Oh I have steadily been reducing my stock over the last six months. To be honest I never held much. These I have now, they are my great joy. I won't part with these no matter how high the price. |
| Financier: | You wouldn't sell them but if I wanted to rent one from you? |
| Florist: | I have never rented anyone a tulip before! Are you throwing a party? |
| Financier: | No, I'm going to cash in on the end of one.<br>I'll give you thirty guilders, take this one and I will have it back to you in three days time. |

| | |
|---|---|
| Financier: | So you may be prepared to insure against their bankruptcy? |
| Florist | Of course. How much? |
| Financier: | Twenty thousand guilders. |
| Florist: | For this cover I would ask one hundred and fifty guilders each month. |
| Financier: | Done. Now, onto the rating of Joost himself, are you sure he is still a good risk? He seemed a bit jumpy to me. I'm thinking of pulling his credit. |
| Florist: | No, no, he is fine. His life has become complicated. The sums are getting large and difficult. Timing is becoming key for him. He is very competitive and driving himself hard. He needs to spend more time in the garden. |
| Financier: | [surprised] Joost has a garden? |
| Florist | Oh he owns huge gardens that he never visits. You would be surprised how much Van Hire is worth. |
| Financier: | And his rating? |
| Florist: | AA |
| Financier: | Just the two As? |
| Florist: | His credit is good. |
| Financier: | But not as good as it was? |
| Florist: | Well, there are many more tulips being imported now, more traders, gardeners trying to grow their own from seed, so supply is strong. On the other side, people have started to come to the limit of what they can easily invest, so demand is softening. I think fairly soon we may see |

## Scene 12 Credit Default Swap (pt 2)
Financier & Florist [Florist's Garden]

In which Financier checks Banker's credit rating,
sells Florist his Credit Default Swaps on the Van Guards
and rents a flower to initiate a short selling project.

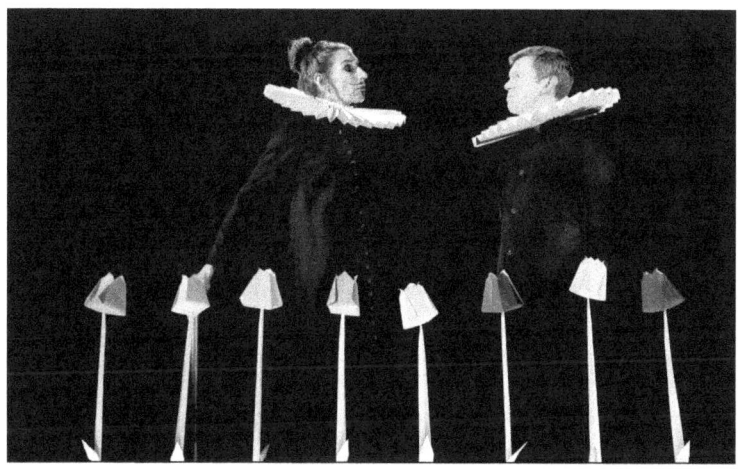

Narrator:   Scene 12: In which Sue's credit rating drops dramatically, but she knows nothing about it.

Financier:  How do you rate the Van Guards?

Florist:    AAA.

Financier:  Van Hire seemed a little anxious about them and their large tulip holding.

Florist:    For the Van Guards tulips are a secondary concern, Pigs are their thing and if Mr Van Hire had spent more time in the restaurants and cafes of Amsterdam he would have picked up rumours of many sensational new pork products that are about to come to market. It is an exciting time to be a pig farmer. For me the Van Guards are AAA.

Financier: You want to take insurance out on them defaulting on their credit.

Banker: Yes, I want to insure their solvency for twenty thousand guilders.

Financier: Fine, one year's insurance against the Van Guards going bankrupt: two hundred guilders a month.

Banker: Two hundred! Those pigs are as fit as you like. I was down there the other weekend, they were zooming around oinking like billy-o. The Van Guards are not going bust. Surely two hundred is too much.

Financier: Then, if they're not going bust, don't insure against them going bust. Two hundred is the rate.

Banker: [reluctantly] A bargain at half the price.

Financier: It will be if those pigs all keel over. Be assured Van Hire I will not pay up if there is a hint of foul play in the farm yard.

Banker: Almost none. Cash is a waste of money. I've got liquid stocks of course and plenty of guaranteed credit lines. I don't want a hedge fund, I'm after a different kind of insurance.

Financier: Such as?

Banker: Insurance.

Financier: On what?

Banker: My investments. Your firm already insures my house and stables and carriages and boats, why not insure my investments.

Financier: You're not making it sound attractive so far. Sell me the idea.

Banker: Right. You know the Van Guards?

Financier: Yes I do. They keep pigs don't they?

Banker: Yes, they're big pig people. Well, they are also among my major creditors and they are investing heavily in my I.O.U. bundles. If their farm fails they may be forced to withdraw their investments and sell their I.O.U. bundles on at a bargain price just to shift them.

Financier: And if they sell their slices at a lower price that automatically reduces the book value of your slices.

Banker: And the value of those slices is what I've used as security to borrow the money to take on these [produces a second bundle]. I'm not worried about it at all, at all, at all; but it would be useful to have some insurance.

Financier: So you wish to take out insurance on the Van Guard pigs?

Banker: No, on the Van Guards not paying me what they owe me.

Banker: Hire.

Financier: I'm sorry Lower?

Banker: Hire, it's Van Hire.

Financier: Of course it is, of course Higher not Lower, us money men, always looking for differential eh?

Banker: Ha ha, yes, quite so, arbritrage! I'm sorry to call on you unexpectedly Adrian, but it is a business meeting of sorts. I have a financial proposition for you.

Financier: You wish to further extend your line of credit?

Banker: No, no thank you (though I might come back to you on that). The truth is, I'm feeling rather exposed in the tulip market and I'm looking for a hedge against it.

Financier: You're losing faith in the current price of tulips?

Banker: NO! No no no no no no no! Not at all. That is a wonderful market; in its infancy! My tulip man Van Eeek is enormously excited by the Tulip. We love the Tulip!

Financier: Then why do you want a hedge?

Banker: Come on Van Tage you know that to hedge is just good practice, the responsible thing to do. Every significant investment should have its hedge and I've come to realise that, although I don't own any tulips many of my creditors do and were they, not that they would, or that I expect them to, in any way lose any significant value, then I have no hedge against that.

Financier: If you want to set up or buy into a hedge fund I can do that for you. How much cash do you have?

the betrothal, by registered attorney, of your daughter to her intended, floating high above the low countries in an outsized wicker hamper slung beneath an enormous bladder filled with heated air, or maybe you have no daughter and choose, with your wife, to travel to a city in the desert devoted to amusement in which, for an entire week, you may sit in front of a flashing, spinning, singing machine pressing low denomination guilders through a narrow aperture in anticipation of aligning four symbols of exotic fruits to herald the return of a small proportion of your low denomination guilders, or you may choose…

Mr. Van Driver? [worker has left]

### Scene 11: Credit Default Swap (Part 1)
Financier & Banker [Financier's Office]

In which Banker insures his loans with the Financier.

Narrator: Scene 11, in which Mrs. O'Reagan, by virtue of having savings in the Halifax Building Society when it demutualises, comes to hold shares in a Bank.

Banker: Adrian Van Tage!

Financier: Van Lower!

reserved only for those I hold in the highest esteem. You can celebrate retirement in grand style, without the shock of a high initial payment.

Worker: We need for nothing.

Banker: There is a difference between needing and wanting.

Worker: We want for nothing.

Banker: Well there's a difference between wanting and wishing.

Worker: Wishing is dreaming. I only dream when I'm sleeping and I never buy anything whilst I'm asleep.

Banker: No, but all the same Ruud, I may call you Ruud mayn't I?

Worker: I prefer Van Driver.

Banker: Mr. Van Driver have you never fancied a machine that through an ingenious concordance of cogs and belts and fans contrives to suck dust from throughout your house and deposit it in a bag for easy disposal, or a contraption that will ingest your soiled linen and after a period of groaning and mechanical shaking, regurgitate such garments clean, if somewhat damp? Consider a further contraption which would ingest that clean yet damp linen and after a further period of whining and a higher pitch of mechanical shaking, release said garments both clean, dry and warm to the touch, or a device that, without the shaking, executes both jobs on your crockery and cutlery, or a bathing tub which will pummel your skin, or a newly paved area beyond the rear of your house on which friends can gather to watch you cook meat-derived products on an open, charcoal fuelled fire, utilising outsized tongs, forks and spatulas, or perhaps you desire a physic might change the shape of your nose outside the randomised context of a public house brawl, or enhance your wife's bust for your mutual gratification, or to finance

### Scene 10: False Need
Worker & Banker [Banker's office]

In which Banker fails to persuade Worker he should buy a tulip.

Narrator: Scene 10: in which twelve items of unsolicited mail fall through Sandra's letterbox, eleven of which are offering her credit and one offers credit to a man who lived in the house eight years before she moved in.

Worker: I am here because I promised both Mr. Van Eeek and Mrs. Van Leasing that I would come and for no other reason. I know all there is to know about tulips and have no desire to hear another word on the subject. So, if you'll excuse me, I'll be making my way. Thank you for your time.

Banker: Wait, wait Mr. Van Driver, thank you for coming and being so candid. I admire a man who knows and speaks his mind. I appreciate investment in tulips is not for everyone but my services go far beyond that.

I have long heard tales of your fiscal responsibility and hear you are on the verge of retirement. In honour of these facts I wish to extend to you a line of credit

Worker: I don't mean that bulb. I mean all these bulbs, all this investment. Forgive me, it is nothing to do with me, but it makes me nervous, this fortune riding on the caprices of nature.

Wife: It is fine Ruud.

Worker: Really? How much of this do you own and how much do you owe?

Wife: We really don't owe that much. Van Hire wouldn't lend to us if he didn't think we could pay him back.

Worker: What does he know?

Wife: The Van Dals owe much more than we do.

Worker: That's their look out, I'm just worried about you.

Wife: That's sweet Ruud, but you really do have a very old fashioned approach to debt.

Worker: I have a sensible approach to debt; don't be in it.

Wife: No Ruud, debt is the only way to get ahead these days. You really should try some trading yourself. You could use the Field Marshal Alverquercq to start you off, I really wouldn't mind. Van Hire would certainly accept it as security so you could borrow a considerable sum against it. You wouldn't have to get too speculative either, with your gardening skills you could make a real go of growing them, then if you sold them yourself, or your wife did, then you would keep all the profit. Ruud, please promise me you will visit Van Hire as soon as you can.

Wife: I was thinking, one of the Field Marshal Alverquercqs looks very much as if it has developed an offset over the winter and I was wondering, if that is the case, whether you would wish to have it?

Worker: Well I…

Wife: No no no, I know what you are going to say and no, it is not too much. It is no less than you deserve Ruud.

Worker: Thank you Ma'am, that would indeed be a… moving gesture, one I and Mrs Van Driver would be very grateful of.

Wife: Then it shall be done and hang the expense. The Van Dals will be horrified but who listens to them? You may be a servant Van Driver, but to us you are family and why shouldn't a servant have a tulip anyway? I believe the Van Guard's man servant has two and not bad specimens either I hear.

Worker: It's not really…

Wife: You shall be the talk of Groningen!

Worker: Our smallholding…

Wife: …shall be graced with a Field Marshal Alverquercq, imagine!

Worker: I am. Ma'am, can you afford this?

Wife: Of course. It is not as if we are buying the bulb for you, clearly that would be absurd! That offset has never appeared on a balance sheet, it has yet to become an asset. What we have never had we shall not miss. It will be yours Ruud and I don't want you to give it a second thought.

investment could really help you stock that small holding with some quality livestock. Ruud, promise me you will consider it at least.

### Scene 9: The Tax Write Off
Wife & Worker [Wife's drawing room]

In which Worker fails to persuade Wife she should be careful.

Narrator: Scene 9, in which Ted Bateman tells his daughter she shouldn't take on a mortgage five times her salary, but is told "it'll be alright".

Wife: Ruud, I've been thinking about your retirement a fair bit recently.

Worker: You and me both Ma'am.

Wife: And I've been thinking about how much we'll miss you and how I'd like us, Mr. Van Leasing and myself, to make a gift to you, as a token of our appreciation of your hard work over the years.

Worker: Well that would be very kind Ma'am.

Florist: Will you be moving away?

Worker: Yes, to be near her family place, up Groningen way.

Florist: So far!

Worker: Yes she travelled down when her original mistress sent her to care for her son as he went through university. She can't wait to be back with her family; smelling the sea and so on. Me, I'm happy anywhere she's happy.

Florist: I know what you mean.
Ruud, is your future provided for?

Worker: I've got my pension, it's nothing to sing about but it will see us through. I've been careful Mr. Van Eeek, unlike some. I've not wasted a guilder since I've been married and I intend to enjoy every second I spend not doing this.

Florist: And you've never thought of spreading your investments? Putting some of your savings into something dynamic and going for some quick growth?

Worker: I have it all in hand thank you Mr. Van Eeek, nice and steady's me.

Florist: And you've never wanted a tulip for yourself?

Worker: Well why would I want one of those?

Florist: For all the reasons everyone else does.

Worker: I can see the Van Leasing's Tulips whenever I wish. Well, whenever I wish and they're blooming. Tell the truth, I've spent so much time tending these that when they come up they'll *feel* like mine.

Florist: I do hear what it is that you are saying Van Driver, but you should really consider it. At this late stage an astute

Narrator: Scene 8, in which employees at R.K.Ferris and Son invest in stakeholder pensions.

Florist: Do you have any idea where he might be?

Worker: No, I don't see much of either of them nowadays.

Florist: And how are you Ruud, still struggling on?

Worker: As ever.

Florist: What do they have you doing now?

Worker: Spreading muck on the garden; pigeon droppings. They're not as easy to find as you might think. Then blue dye on the soil. I can't keep up with this modern thinking. What's wrong with horse shit and flowers the colour that nature intended?

Florist: I'm afraid some of that is my fault Ruud.

Worker: Well thank you kindly Sir. Please watch what you say in future. Maybe the next fad should be for the wild pasture look without human intervention.

Florist: Very good Ruud, very good!

Worker: Me, I can't wait to be out of it.

Florist: How long now?

Worker: Three months and counting down. Not long after this lot have come into bloom.

Florist: What are your plans?

Worker: A smallholding and no one to answer to but myself and the wife, that's if we can recall what each other looks like.

Florist: Interesting.

Banker: Yes, they're accusing me of discrimination but if they believe this they don't understand me very well.

Florist: Indeed.

Banker A servant's money is as good as a merchant's money in my hand, so long as they are minted form the same ore. Anyway, it could mark a big expansion of the market and I need some cash for that.

Florist: Surely these new I.O.U.s will be more vulnerable to default?

Banker: True, but with tulip prices constantly rising if they fail to pay, ownership of the flower defaults to me.

### Scene 8: The Pension (Pt. 1)
Florist & Worker [Florist's Garden]

In which Florist fails to persuade Worker he too should buy a tulip.

Florist: That sounds fair. Now, let me select my third.

Banker: No, it doesn't work like that. It's a package, we slice it like this [motions vertically] not like this [motions horizontally] so it all evens out, the risk, reward and cashflow.

Florist: That sounds very complicated.

Banker: Not at all, you're just buying a share in the package.

Florist: Then you will at least let me look at who will end up owing me money.

Banker: Of course, though it is confidential and you mustn't pass it on.

Florist: I can't promise that, if these same people also owe someone else money that we don't know about then maybe they will pay them before us.

Banker: Well just don't broadcast it too widely then.

Florist: Fine. This looks good. Yes, you have done well there. They are all exemplary citizens, most own houses, estates, inheritances. I have no problem with these people's honour. AAA I would say.

Banker: So the seven thousand?

Florist: I shall get it at once. Do you have plans for it?

Banker: Van Ish is pressurising me to pay him some money I owe him.

Florist: Really?

Banker But I may stall him. The city authorities are putting me under some moral pressure to help our less advantaged citizens get a foot on the tulip ladder.

owns what?

Florist: I have, but once the people I have sold the bulbs to in turn sell them on to third parties and hence even to fourth or fifth parties I am not always kept abreast of who has claim to what.

Banker: It sounds like a job for the lawyers. Now listen Van Eeek, I'm going to cut to it. As you know this tulip business has been going very well. You've been making a decent bit of money from the front end of it I imagine. I wonder if you fancy making some money off the back end too?

Florist: How do you mean, flower arranging?

Banker: No, by buying some of these off me.

Florist: I.O.U.s?

Banker: Yes, I have twenty thousand guilders of loans here, all due to be paid off in the next two years, I'm due to clear two thousand guilder's interest on them in that time but there's demand out there that I now haven't got the cash to meet.

Florist: That sounds interesting but I don't have twenty thousand.

Banker: How about coming in for half.

Florist: I could do a third.

Banker: That would be fantastic, seven thousand for a third of the I.O.U.s...

Florist: Six thousand six hundred and sixty six surely?

Banker: I did all the work originating the I.O.U.s dealing with all the paper work. I need my cut, three hundred and thirty is barely a slice.

### Scene 7: Mortgage Backed Securities.
Florist & Banker [Florist's Garden]

In which banker sells bundles of I.O.U.s to the Florist and explains he is under pressure to extend the scope of tulip ownership.

Narrator: Scene 7, in which Citibank buys a tranche of triple A rated mortgage backed securities.

Banker: Ah, my dear Van Eeek

Florist: Van Hire, how good to see you. Have you come to admire the garden?

Banker: No, though I'm sure it's a wonder.

Florist: At the moment it is mostly all underground. It's a bit awkward, I'm trying to sell the house but the contract with regards to the garden is a bit complicated. Of course the contents are not part of the sale but we can't disturb any of the bulbs until after the blooming.

Banker: I imagine you've been keeping a good record of who

be the tulip.

If you had real wealth Mr. Van Leasing what interest would you pursue?

Husband: I should like to collect paintings, such as those by Mr. Rembrandt.

Banker: There you are you see, exactly the eccentric whim that the wealthy are allowed... no, are *expected* to indulge themselves in. Secure your future with tulips Mr. Van Leasing and indulge in whatever passing fad gives you pleasure.

Do you or any close relatives have any assets you may be able to use as security towards a larger loan and more bulbs?

Husband: Well, there is our house I suppose, and my mother does have a small quantity of jewellery that my father gave her over the years.

Husband: Van Eeek has been very helpful. He is very enthusiastic about the whole field of tulips. I'm so pleased he introduced us to them. We will have the delight of their flowers whilst they are also securing our financial future.

Banker: It is reassuring to know your wealth is growing in the soil whilst you go about you daily business. Once you have this second bulb you should find it easier to raise money for investing in a third. Each bulb will be progressively easier to finance and all the time your wealth and your garden will be growing more impressive.

It just seems a shame, with the market as it is and with you and your wife ahead of the game as you are, that you might miss out by, dare I say it, not being ambitious enough.

Husband: You think we've been too cautious?

Banker: No, not at all. It's just, I don't want you, in a few years time, when you look back on this moment, to think "I wish I had grasped that opportunity firmly with both hands, not just limply with one". If now you had four or even six bulbs working for you rather than just two consider the mathematics of that scenario. Six bulbs worth just a single guilder each doubling in value every season as seems the current rate; in five doublings (a little over a year) your six guilders will have become almost two hundred whilst your two guilders will now be a little over sixty. Both excellent returns, don't get me wrong, but one hundred and forty guilders extra for in initial investment of just four extra, who wouldn't want to find the four extra at the start? These returns dwarf the original investment so rapidly that what seems a large sum to borrow now will appear a trifle then. For the want of this trifle at the start you may be sacrificing the kind of wealth that will allow you to follow whatever interest takes you, just as the wealthy merchants do now. Indeed you will be a wealthy merchant and your commodity will

### Scene 6: Equity Release
Husband & Banker [Banker's Office]

In which husband asks to borrow more money
to buy more tulips and other items

Narrator: Scene 6, in which Sue and Mark re-mortgage their house in order to extend the kitchen.

Banker: Then the price you paid for the bulb was how much?

Husband: 150 guilders.

Banker: Very good. Well I have a note from Van Eeek that says that same bulb is now worth 200 guilders, so you have fifty guilders extra security there to add to the forty guilder deposit which was the off-set option your wife sold that friend of Van Eeek's, plus you have already paid off a portion of the debt on your original bulb so we can add that sum to the security. I would say on this second bulb, with that deposit and those extra securities, I could lend you another 250 guilders, provided of course the quality of your purchase is approved by Van Eeek.

|         | be gaining in value at a similar rate to your offset. |
|---------|---|
| Wife:   | And which variety would you recommend? Forty guilders won't get us much. |
| Florist: | No, forty guilders won't but it is a decent down payment. |
| Wife:   | And what about security? We have already pledged the peacock to Van Hire. |
| Florist: | Listen, between you and me, Mr. Van Hire is very keen on this tulip trade and keen to get a good slice of the business connected with it. I'm sure he can sort something out for you. |
| Wife:   | We could buy another Van Leyden. Two together would look magnificent. |
| Florist: | They would, but I would recommend diversifying your portfolio. |
| Wife:   | Meaning? |
| Florist: | Well with one Van Leyden you could balance it with a Triumph or an Ambassador, which is just becoming a popular variety but difficult to get hold of. You may consider buying a number of lesser bulbs, they are easier to sell on when the time comes, but unless one develops an offset or breaks, their return would be modest compared to the high value pieces, such as this one. The Sensation, it is exceptionally rare, prone to breaking with occasional double flowers. If you purchased it out of season and were prepared to wait, paying interest whilst the bulb is beneath the ground in someone else's garden, you could possibly stretch to the Sensation, king of all tulips. |

Florist: The Van Leyden is a beautiful strain as it is and who knows, yours may yet mutate. If you wish to encourage this you should instruct your man to add pigeon dung to your soil around the bulbs along with perhaps a blue dye such as is used in the fabric trade.

Wife: Van Eeek, do you think our purchase of the Root Van Leyden was unwise?

Florist: No, no indeed. The price of all tulips has risen in recent months and the Van Leyden at a rate faster than most. You were wise to get in early and if, as you believe, an off-set really is developing then that is magnificent news. I know a gentleman who would be willing to pay you a significant sum in order to have the option of buying that off-set at an agreed price from you in the future.

Wife: I'm sorry, I don't understand.

Florist: We agree now on a price at which you will be willing to sell your bulb's off-set in say, six months time. My client will give you forty guilders in order to have first refusal at that price when the time comes.

Wife: And if the offset doesn't develop as we hope it will?

Florist: Then you keep your forty guilders.

Wife: And if, as you suggest, the price of these bulbs continues to rise and we have set our off-set price too low?

Florist: Then my client has a bargain and, if he chooses to sell it on, a profit. That is your gamble and his. But remember, if you lose that gamble then you may gain in other ways.

Wife: How so?

Florist: You can hedge against escalating prices by investing the forty guilder option fee on bulbs, which will themselves

## Scene 5: Futures Trading
Florist & Wife [Florist's Drawing Room]

In which Wife admires more flowers and hears that prices are rising.

Narrator: Scene 5, in which Joan asks how her gas bill is going up when the wholesale price of gas is coming down.

[Florist and Wife admiring a painting]

Wife: ...and this flaming and the ragged edges of the petals, this is the artist making fanciful with his subject?

Florist: No Madam, this is as close a likeness of the subject as you could wish to imagine. The exquisite ragged edges are a mutation we floristines call breaking. If the tulip were to have a scent I warrant this canvas would be wreathed in it.

Wife: Somehow it makes our Root Van Leyden appear positively dowdy in its colouring and common in its shape.

| | caring for her every need. |
|---|---|
| Worker: | Slave to a plant. |
| Husband: | A servant to me more correctly; if that is still your wish? |
| Worker: | Hardly my wish Sir, but my reality. Do you want me to bury your treasure? |
| Husband: | Not yet. Van Eeek says to keep it in the dry air until September, then plant it out over the winter and wait for the bloom in Spring. |
| Worker: | Very well Sir and until then? |
| Husband: | I will keep it under lock and key. You know Van Driver you might consider getting yourself a tulip eventually. Some of the more common strains are really quite affordable. |
| Worker: | Whose measure of affordability is this we are talking about now, Sir? |

| | |
|---|---|
| Worker: | Very nice. |
| Husband: | It should be. |
| Worker: | You saw it bloom? |
| Husband: | I saw the catalogue painting. |
| Worker: | But not the bloom? |
| Husband: | It is a recent import. A contact of Van Eeek's. We were going to get one of his before it came into bloom this year, but you get more for your guilder post-bloom, the waiting time. It should be truly spectacular. I am assured it is the only one of its kind in Haarlem, if not the country. |
| Worker: | I'm impressed. How much did it cost? |
| Husband: | It was 150 guilders. |
| Worker: | Pardon? |
| Husband: | That is a just price for a bulb of this rarity and beauty. |
| Worker: | A just price! How long does it bloom for? |
| Husband: | Our guess? A fortnight. |
| Worker: | Fourteen days for 150 guilders… that's… more that ten guilders each day! I wish I was worth as much. |
| Husband: | Merit is measured differentially Van Driver. |
| Worker: | Evidently. Well, I hope you can feast your eyes enough and that rain does not spoil your viewing, or slugs feast on her, or a late frost ruin her, or aphids pox her, or a jealous neighbour spirit her away or... |
| Husband: | Don't worry Van Driver, *you* will be tending this beauty; |

## Scene 4: The Market
Husband & Worker [Husband's Garden]

In which a tulip bulb is displayed and Worker is shocked at its price.

Narrator: Scene 4, in which Richard and Tony watch *Property Ladder* together.

Worker: Nice shallot.

Husband: Do you mind! It's not a shallot, it's a tulip bulb and before you ask, no, you don't eat tulips; you admire them. They are very beautiful.

Worker: Don't worry, I know all about tulips, the latest wonder from the East, turning everyone's heads it seems. Someone is making a pretty guilder on this fashion.

Husband: Do be careful!

Worker: What kind is she?

Husband: That, is 515 azen of fine Gheel Ende Root Van Leyden, its flower will be finely striped, red and yellow.

|         | the people who lend to me, their rate changes. I must pass on the cost or I lose money. The money is there, it is your choice. |
|---------|---|
| Wife:   | And if I say 'yes' then it is twelve lots of twelve and we are done? |
| Banker: | It is twelve guilders a month unless the rate changes then it could be less or it could be more. |
| Wife:   | You want me to guarantee that I can pay but you are not prepared to say how much you will charge, how can that be sensible? |
| Banker: | You need to have some margin, some slack, you shouldn't push to your limit. If you are worried then don't take the loan, don't buy the flower. I tell you what I can do to give you peace of mind, if you pay me thirteen guilders each month then I promise that this rate will not change for the first six months, from then on you pay whatever the rate is. Or, I could guarantee you thirteen and a half guilders for the entire course of the loan. |
| Wife:   | What do you think the chances of the rate going up above thirteen and a half are? |
| Banker: | All I can say is that twelve is a record, we have never been above twelve to go to thirteen would be historic. |
| Wife:   | OK twelve it is and let's trust to luck. |
| Banker: | Good, I just need your signature on the I.O.U.. |

Wife: It is, we've had it valued.

Banker: But it's about to flower, what happens if in six months time, when it's just a bulb in the ground, you default and I need to raise my money? It won't be worth that money then.

Wife: It will and anyway you will already have had sixty guilders off us. It would certainly be worth more than the remaining forty guilders.

Banker: I have no guarantee of that. I know nothing of flowers. I am worried. Your earnings are not high. I am not prepared to risk it.

Wife: If I could find you something else of value, something to pledge against the loan in addition to the tulip?

Banker: Then of course we could talk again.

Wife: Thank you [wife leaves and after a significant pause returns with a peacock] How about this? It is worth fifty guilders. You may call on this as security.

Banker: Good. I am prepared to take this and the tulip itself as security if you will pay me back twelve guilders a month for the year.

Wife: Twelve? I thought it was ten!

Banker: My rates have risen.

Wife: Twelve is too much.

Banker: Twelve is the rate.

Wife: Can't you do any better than that for me?

Banker: I am sorry, that is the rate. It changes, my costs fluctuate,

## Scene 3: The Mortgage
Wife & Banker [Banker's Office]

In which a loan is agreed, security offered, an I.O.U. written and interest paid.

Narrator: Scene 3: in which Denise gets her first mortgage and takes it to the limit.

Banker: You pay me back ten guilders a month for a year.

Wife: Yes.

Banker: Until then the tulip is mine not yours, you understand?

Wife: Yes.

Banker: You don't pay me one month and I have the right to sell that tulip in order to get my money back.

Wife: Yes.

Banker: And if the flower isn't worth what I've leant you?

Wife: Then we shall have to save.

Husband: Yes, we could save. But by the time we have that kind of money the flowers will have withered, even those that are now budding.

Wife: Then we shall have to buy one next year.

Husband: But if this is a bargain as you say, Van Eeek is no fool, he is generous perhaps but he didn't make his money by accident. Who knows what his prices might be next year? I say we should buy now.

Wife: I am not asking Van Eeek for credit. I wouldn't feel comfortable being in his debt. Who knows what his interest might be?

Husband: You're right, I know of his interests too well. We need someone a bit more distant, disinterested.

Wife: How about Van Hire? I have heard he lends money on reasonable terms.

Husband: Perfect!

Wife: Oh Husband, isn't this fantastic! We are going to have our very own tulip. What colour should we have?

Husband: That depends on how much Van Hire is willing to loan us. Remember we must not stretch ourselves too far. I am still paying Van Essa for the peacock.

Wife: Eight!

Husband: Yes, two blooming, five budding and one he has picked.

Wife: He's picked one! What decadence! Do you know how much they cost?

Husband: I know exactly: fifteen guilders for a red one, thirteen for a yellow.

Wife: That's a good deal, who did he get them from at that price?

Husband: No, that's his price for us. It took some work to get him to quote at all. He is reluctant to sell. Eventually I called in our friendship and he quoted those prices saying it was a 'Special Friendship Rate'. I had thought he was having me on or trying to pull a stunt but clearly he wasn't.

Wife: Darling, that is more than a fair price, Van Eeek is a generous man.

Husband: It's still preposterous.

Wife: If it were a cut flower I would agree with you but it's not, it is a bulb, it will flower again next year and the year after that; for ever if we tend it well. Each year that goes by that flower will become more of a bargain. If it were to grow an offset then that would effectively halve our price again. We would then have two flowers for the price of one and a cheap one at that. In a further few years if both were to produce offsets that would be four, then eight, sixteen, thirty two… need I go on?

I think we should buy one.

Husband: Well, if it's no longer preposterous and has even become a bargain, well then thirteen is still more guilders than we have or can hope to have in the near future.

## Scene 2: Credit
Wife & Husband [Their Garden]

In which the couple discuss the merits of tulips, decide they wish to buy one and do not wish to wait.

Narrator: Scene 2: in which Sandra and Tony discuss buying a sofa on h.p.

Wife: Ah Husband, I have just come over from the Van Guards and saw the most extraordinary thing there, a flower with a vividness of colour that I have never seen before. Admittedly it had no fragrance and apparently the bulbs taste foul even when fried in butter, but the colours! They're from the East you know. They're terribly difficult to get hold of. The Van Guards have a relation in the silk trade. You really should see them.

Husband: Were they tulips?

Wife: That's them! How did you know? Have you... [seen them]

Husband: Van Eeek has one, actually he has eight.

Husband: Listen Van Eeek. I understand your reluctance to part with too many of your wonderful Tulips and endanger your future supplies, but surely seven is as good as eight and I am only next door and if I were prepared to pay you something, as a token of my gratitude…

Florist: No, Van Leasing I'm afraid I cannot. You can always admire my Tulips over the fence.

Husband: From afar?

Florist: What am I saying? We are friends! I'm too harsh. Of course you can come round at any time. You can let yourself in. I shall give you a key to the gate. You can gaze at my flowers at any time, for as long as you wish, for looking at them will not wear them out.

Husband: How much might one cost?

Florist: You can look at them all you wish at any time for no charge. I imagine you can even see them from your second floor window.

Husband: I know, I know… but I do rather feel I need to *have* rather than to merely *see* one of these magnificent blooms.

|  | insert it? |
|---|---|
| Florist: | You look at it. |
| Husband: | How so? |
| Florist: | It is beautiful. You look at it. You admire it. It is a Tulip. |
| Husband: | It is indeed beautiful. How did you come by it? |
| Florist: | It is from Turkey or thereabouts. I have a man who brings me objects of curiosity and fascination, along with my other stock. In those parts men wear great swirls of cloth around their heads and tuck one of these, a Tulip, at the front. He thought I would like it and I do, very much. |
| Husband: | I do too, very much, like it. Do you have many more? |
| Florist: | There are another seven in my garden, two in bloom and five budding that I have high hopes for. |
| Husband: | Seven you say. Five budding. Van Eeek, you and I, we share a fascination with horticulture would you not say? We have been neighbours since the canal was dug and these buildings built? We have shared so much over those years, in fortune both good and ill would you not say? |
| Florist: | Van Leasing, what is it? |
| Husband: | Van Eeek, as you have seven in the ground and one in hand, considering you have eight and I have none, would you give me one of your budding tulips? |
| Florist: | My dear friend of course, of course, of course I would have, but not now. It is too late. I have already given away half my Tulips to fellow floristines across the country. I must retain a stock. |

## Scene 1: Ownership
Husband & Florist [Florist's Garden]

In which Husband sees Florist's tulips and decides he must buy one.

Narrator:   Scene 1: in which seeing is not enough.

Husband:    Ah Van Eeek I was just going to...
            I say, what a flower! What flower is that?

Florist:    [tulip held high] This, is a tulip.

Husband:    Magnificent, what does it taste of?

Florist:    I don't know; I've never tasted it.

Husband:    The roots then, they are sweet perhaps?

Florist:    No, it is not to taste, but to sooth the eye and calm the spirit.

Husband:    Ah, I see, one of those, it is medicinal. Do you infuse it or

He had the ear of the rich and powerful
He'd offices in twenty five cities and towns
And a mansion in the Home Counties

One day a man even richer than Fred was
Said he'd buy his company for gazillions
But Fred shook his head, said no, no, no, no
My widget's worth far more than that

One day on his yacht, thinking life got no better
A phone call came through from accounts
Every home out there had got his widget
There was no-one left now to buy them

So Fred went back to the bank for some money
With a smile I'm worth millions he said
I've offices in twenty five cities you know
And a workforce of a thousand and two

But the bank shook their heads and said no no
No-one wants what you've got to sell
We're sorry Mr Frederick Freddy O'Toole
You're not worth the paper you're written on

Now Fred's a sole trader from his garden shed
In the grounds of his Home Counties mansion
The roof leaks, wind rattles the windows
And he works hard to put food on the table

EPILOGUE
What is a man worth?
When he has it all then loses it all
What is a man worth?
When no-one's prepared to pay

What is he worth when he first sees the light?
And what is he worth when he blinks his last
What is a man worth?
And who is it doing the counting?

## Prologue: The Just Price Of Flowers

[Before each scene Narrator hangs a sign announcing its title]

Narrator: The Just Price of Flowers

[Song]

There once was a young man called Frederick
That's Frederick 'Freddy' O'Toole
He was born in a back street two up two down
Shared a bed with six brothers and sisters

His mum worked hard to put food on the table
The roof leaked, wind rattled the windows
So Fred determined his life would be better
That he would go off and make millions

So Fred had a brilliant idea one day
A creation to change his world and ours
He invented a very special device
A widget to make life much easier

Now having a dream is one thing you know
But with no cash Fred's couldn't come true
So one day he borrowed his brothers old suit
Combed his hair flat, went down to the bank

Fred proudly showed the bankers his widget
Told them the whole world would want to buy one
The bankers said yes you are right course they will
Shook Freddy's hand and lent him some money

With this loan Fred started building his widgets
And soon every home wanted one
They started to sell all over like hot cakes
And our Freddy started making his millions

All that Fred touched seemed to turn into money

## Contents:

| | | | |
|---|---|---|---|
| Prologue (Song) | | Narrator | 1 |
| Scene | 1 | Husband & Florist | 3 |
| Scene | 2 | Husband & Wife | 6 |
| Scene | 3 | Banker & Wife | 9 |
| Scene | 4 | Husband & Worker | 12 |
| Scene | 5 | Wife & Florist | 15 |
| Scene | 6 | Banker & Husband | 18 |
| Scene | 7 | Florist & Banker | 21 |
| Scene | 8 | Worker & Florist | 24 |
| Scene | 9 | Worker & Wife | 27 |
| Scene | 10 | Worker & Banker | 30 |
| Scene | 11 | Financier & Banker | 32 |
| Scene | 12 | Financier & Florist | 36 |
| Scene | 13 | Financier & Husband | 39 |
| Scene | 14 | Financier & Wife | 42 |
| Song | | Everyone | 44 |
| Scene | 15 | Husband, Wife & Banker | 46 |
| Scene | 16 | Banker Florist & Worker | 48 |
| Scene | 17 | Banker, Financier & Worker | 50 |
| Scene | 18 | Banker, Financier & Florist | 53 |
| Scene | 19 | Banker | 56 |
| Scene | 20 | Wife, Husband & Florist | 57 |
| Scene | 21 | Worker & Financier | 59 |
| Song (Reprise) | | Everyone | 61 |
| Credits | | | 62 |